LORD OF
THE YOUNG CROWD

Dan

May you live a
Joy-filled life in
our Lord.

Rev. Leighland Johnson
May 21, 1972

LORD
OF THE
YOUNG CROWD

ROY G. GESCH

Concordia Publishing House
St. Louis   London

Concordia Publishing House, St. Louis, Missouri
Concordia Publishing House Ltd., London, E. C. 1
Copyright © 1971 Concordia Publishing House
Library of Congress Catalog Card No. 72-162531
International Standard Book No. 0-570-03126-5

MANUFACTURED IN THE UNITED STATES OF AMERICA

To Sherri and Elli

CONTENTS

I
My God and I

II
Discovering Me

III
Family, Friends, and School

IV
For Everything There Is a Time

PREFACE

You, the youth of now, perhaps more than young people of any previous generation, are being trained and encouraged to think, to think for yourself, and to speak out your thoughts honestly.

It is important that you do so also in prayer.

These short prayers are not meant to put words in your mouth. They are intended rather to get you started in being truly yourself as you speak to your heavenly Father.

It is my hope that they will also keep you mindful that God does answer prayer and that He has answers for your questions, doubts, and needs — answers that necessarily lie less in man and limited human wisdom, more in the written Word and Christ, the living Word.

Develop the habit of honest prayer, remembering, as Jesus promised, that the asker receives, the seeker finds, and the knocker has doors opened to him.

ROY G. GESCH

I

*My God
and I*

Lord of the Teen-Ager

Lord Jesus, it means a lot to me to know that You were also once a teen-ager.

You know what it's like — to be treated like a child when you're really not a child; to try to get accepted as an adult when you're really not adult.

You know what is in the young heart. You know my true longings and feelings, even those I do not recognize or know how to express.

When I come to You, as I do now, I know You're not judging me by what other young people are doing, or even by what others think of me.

And I know You're not laughing or shaking Your head at me.

You, who understand me so well, help me understand myself. Keep me aware of Your love and what I can become in that love.

I thank You for coming to be eternal Friend and Savior of all mankind — also of us teen-agers.

Do I Know You?

Great God, do I know You?

You know me — but do I know You?

I know that You are one God, one Lord, and I know about Father, Son, and Holy Spirit — but do I really know You?

I know how You made us and how You take care of us — but do I really know You?

I know about Christ's saving love, His miracles and teachings, His dying for us, His victory over death and hell, and that He will come again to judge — but do I really know You?

I know of the Spirit's gifts, of how He uses Your Word of truth to bring us to You and life — but do I really know You?

Like they say, "It's not what you know but *who* you know." Knowing a lot about You isn't the same as really knowing You.

Dear God, help me know You — that knowing You, I may also believe in You — and believing, I may love You with all my heart — and loving You, I may serve You with all my life.

My Father

Father, I hope it shows that I think You're the greatest!

It's really exciting to know that You're not just some vague Someone somewhere way out there — way out where we can hardly reach.

It's good to know You as my personal Friend and to know that when I pray, You hear and understand.

But Lord, I don't want it to be a buddy-buddy feeling. I want and need to know You above all as my Father — a Father who knows even what I don't tell — a Father who forgives instead of overlooks — a Father who let Jesus go to bat for me when Satan's whole team was out on the field to get me — a Father who seeks only my good.

Father, I want to love You with all my heart. Give me such love.

I want to trust You so much that I'd be willing to stake everything on every word You've said. Give me such faith.

And I want my worship to show I respect You. Most kids are proud of their dads. Well, I'd like the whole world to know that there never has been nor will there ever be One greater than You, my Father.

My Promise

Father, I've reached a point in my life where I'm ready to make an important decision and promise to You.

My parents and others did a lot of my deciding and promising for me in the past. But now I'm old enough to think and speak for myself.

Through Your Word I've come to know quite a bit about You and Your love. I've also come to know a bit about myself and how much I really need You.

I've come to know Jesus — not only as a perfect Model to follow, but also as Your Son sent to be my Way to heaven. And in Your goodness You've brought me to where I really believe this, and trust You and what You've said.

So I'm stating myself. I'd like it to be known that I am Yours and that I'd like You to take over my whole life.

I really want to follow You and do what You want me to do. I want to be faithful to You through every day of my life.

I want to be — but I know I could never make it without Your help. So help me, Father! You, who can never break a promise, help me keep mine.

Fill Me Up!

Dearest Savior, when I think of all You've done for me, I want to do so much for You.

I want to — but too often my enthusiasm fizzles out before I actually get anything done.

Maybe I'm like an electric motor that's able to turn out great power — but isn't plugged in.

Or a souped-up sports car that's capable of high performance — but isn't getting the fuel it needs.

Lord Jesus, don't let me forget that great things happen when You work through us; but also that we can't work by ourselves.

It's Your life, Your power. Like You put it, "Without Me you can do nothing."

Lord, make my first concern that I'm plugged in to You. Keep the fuel line open. Give me the will to let You, through Your Word, fill me up before I try to hit the road.

Love

Dear Jesus, so many of the now songs say we should put more love into our living.

That's right, isn't it? There's nothing the world needs more than real love. I guess it's always been that way.

Some starve, while others waste. Some struggle, while others refuse to lift a finger. Some take advantage of others and selfishly get ahead at others' expense.

Lord, how can we put more love into life? Not by breeding hate and violence, and screaming insults. That's for sure!

It seems to me You have the only real answer, Jesus. You just loved! You didn't talk about it— You did it! You loved enough to give Your whole life for others. You loved not only Your closest friends and other lovable people, but everyone. And You didn't wait for them to love You first. You took the lead.

Now I hear You saying to me and to us all: "Love one another, as I have loved You."

Give me a love like Yours, dear Lord. Even if others don't respond to it, let me keep loving. It has to be the only way.

Trust

Dear Savior, when I think of all You've done for us, I get excited about all the things I want to do as an alive Christian.

It's hard to be told, then, that I must first of all learn to sit back and put my trust in You.

Somehow it seems it ought to depend on me — on my choice, my strength, my abilities, my doing.

I guess what I need to learn is like what we learn in water-skiing. There's nothing we can do to get on top of the water or skim swiftly across it.

All we can do is hold on and lie back. The driver of the boat does it all. He pulls us up and on. And the minute we let go and try things on our own, down we go.

Lord Jesus, teach me how to put my trust in You in just that way. Your life, Your power, Your love, Your wisdom can do great things through me. But don't let me forget that the minute I let go of You and try to go it on my own, the direction is down.

Mountaintops

O Jesus, what a comedown for Peter, James, and John, to leave the mountain where they saw You in all Your glory! That was the most wonderful thing they could have seen short of heaven.

Then to have to leave it, and come back down to dust and sweat and tears and tiredness and ordinariness—that must have been almost too much!

I guess we've all had some mountaintop experience, enough to give us a taste of what it's like.

A youth retreat, where everything centered around You, and we really felt close to You and one another. A church service, where beautiful music or the minister's way of opening up Your Word or Your personal touch in Communion made us sense Your glory and love as never before. It really doesn't matter much what it was as long as it was a mountaintop for us.

How hard it is to leave it—to tangle again with the daily grind of the plains! But we must, I guess, as we live here and now for You, Christ.

I thank You for those mountaintops. They may be relatively few, but they keep us going.

I thank You also that by Your grace and love, by Your life and death and promise, ours is a mountaintop eternity.

Lead Me

"Send out Thy light and Thy truth; let them lead me."

Father, I've read of birds that were shipped half around the world. When they were released, they instinctively set their course and found their way home even though it meant flying thousands of unfamiliar miles over water and land.

I don't have such an unfailing sense of direction.

When I set out for some place I've never seen before, I need help. I check maps and ask others where it is and how to get there.

Lord, send Your Spirit to guide me through life. I have many a mile to walk before my journey is ended. There are many paths that lead in all directions.

So I look to You to keep me on the right way, that I may finally reach my heavenly home, not just a dead end.

Teach me how to read Your Word-map so I can see Jesus as the Way, and confidently go that way.

When others urge me to other paths, and dangers and temptations threaten to change my course, keep me on the Christ-way.

For so I shall reach home at last.

The Hang-Up of Sin

Dear Jesus, how do I get control of myself?

I really do want to be a true Christian. I know and appreciate all You have done for me. I realize that it's by Your grace, by the Spirit's power, that I am Your redeemed and born-again child.

But no matter how I try to be like You, I find myself failing. I try to follow You and suddenly find myself on other paths.

I know the apostle Paul also complained about doing what he didn't want to do and not doing what he should. I know St. John said that anyone who thinks he doesn't sin is deceiving himself.

But the fact that others, even great Christian leaders, had the same problem, doesn't make me feel better.

I'm letting You down. That matters.

Lord Jesus, forgive me. Make my life more consistent with my faith.

Who Says So?

O Holy Spirit, Jesus promised that You would teach us all things. Teach me, for I get so confused.

It seems everybody has his own ideas about what's true or false, and what's right and wrong. And they make me feel as if I don't know anything unless I see things their way.

Even when it comes to things that were supposed to have happened before man was on this earth or what happens after death, they act as if they know it all.

But how can they? Really, only You can. You were there, even as You are now and always will be.

Give me the kind of courage to hold on to Your Word. Help me to know by faith. When others challenge, ''Who says so?'' make me strong enough to speak up, ''God says so!'' and to do it without feeling embarrassed about my faith.

The greatest Christians of all times were those who stood firmly on ''Thus saith the Lord!'' Let me be such a Christian in my day.

I Have Ears

I remember, Jesus, how often You said, "He who has ears to hear, let him hear."

I have ears, Lord! But I'm afraid there are times when I, like many others, don't hear so well.

Oh, the sound comes through all right. But I turn it down. I tune out the message.

I guess that's my way of saying, "I'm not interested." And that bothers me. How can I say that to You?

"He who is of God hears the words of God; the reason why you do not hear them is that you are not of God," You once said.

That's really hitting hard, Lord! But whether I like to face up to it or not, it's true!

When my Bible collects dust . . . when I go to church mostly because I have to . . . when I drag my feet at learning Your Word . . . and don't practice what You preach—maybe I'd better ask, "Am I really Yours?" I claim to be. But am I?

You've given me ears. Lord, help me hear.

We Are the Church

Lord Jesus, sometimes it's a little hard to get the idea that we are the church and to see it as You mean it.

Being the church is so often confused with fun nights and swim parties and burger bashes . . . or attendance records and awards . . . or weeding the lawn or painting the parish hall as youth's role in church.

Maybe that's why I sometimes feel out of it. I don't always fit that picture. I don't make that scene.

Lord Jesus, we need Your Spirit to get through to us. Show us how, by faith, we are the church, and what it means to have You as our Head, and to be Your body. Show us how to be living, active members of Your body—tongues that speak for You, eyes that seek for You, hands that work for You, legs that run for You, hearts that love for You.

And show us now, Jesus, before our youth slips away.

Ideals?

Father, some of my friends give me no peace.
They say I'm being unrealistic, that I have to learn
to live in the world the way it is and adjust to its
standards. They say I must give up a few ideals,
lower and compromise a few principles, or I'll
never get along. They say it's perfectly all right
that I do so — there just is no other way. Otherwise
I'll be a square peg in a round hole — and they do
mean square.

They say . . . oh, what's the matter with me? It's
what You say that should come first with me.

Don't let their opinions cause me to sell out my
faith or ideals. When they're dead and gone,
You'll still be God and Lord.

If anybody is going to change anybody, help me
change them.

The Name of the Game

I know, Father, that the rules by which one plays are determined by the game he is playing. It's pretty important to know the name of the game.

It's weird even to think of trying baseball rules on water polo or boxing regulations on a football game. It doesn't make sense. Nothing applies. Rules are necessary, but they have to be tailored to the game.

Father, do not let me overlook how true that is in all of life!

Some think that they can keep making up new rules as they go along, no matter what the name of the game is. They even play at being a Christian that way — "my rules or no rules!"

I know I can't do that, Father. No matter how much rules may vary in other things, they are unwaveringly clear here. The way You've drawn them up and explained them is good.

Whether You ask us to believe in the Lord Jesus Christ or to live our faith by Your Commandments — that's it! That's where it stands! Those are the rules by which we win!

Regardless of how others may think things should be, give me the peace and strength of knowing that Your way is right.

God's Dropouts?

Lord Jesus, they say the teen years are a time of tremendous dropout in the church. I guess there's no denying it. But why should it be?

Tired of routines, of learning the same old lessons? Looking for new kinds of truth? Parental pressure has eased? Thinking for ourselves?

Somehow, none of that makes sense. Do any of these really have anything to do with what it's all about? with faith? with being a Christian?

I remember the young man who thought of following You but turned sorrowfully away. We always say he loved his wealth too much. It got in the way, between him and You. But couldn't it also be that he never really knew You, Lord Jesus?

I wonder if the big problem isn't that so many who slip away never really knew You. Maybe they knew You with the mind but not with the heart. Not by faith. Maybe they're not dropping out. Maybe they've never been in. Maybe they've been in a church but not in You.

Lord, fill us all with real faith. Show us how to use each moment well in living and sharing this faith so that neither we nor others whom we can reach may lose all by losing You.

A Heart Full of Others

Dear Jesus, help me love others the way You love us all. Not just with love feelings and love words, but love action. For surely that's the real test and proof of love.

Let me love in action today. Too often I plan to live my love tomorrow, and it never happens.

There was this TV commercial: a little black child . . . a skeleton with thin leathery skin wrapped loosely around him . . . stomach bloated . . . big eyes hollow and almost dead. The voice came through: "There's no way you can help this child. He'll be dead before you can do anything. But you can help thousands of others who are starving."

That kind of thing really gets me. A little kid like that, and you want to help him so much. But it's too late.

Lord Jesus, fill my heart with people. Not just my friends and family. Others. With everyone who needs my love.

Let me love them now, before it's too late for them. Whether it's sending food for an empty stomach or sharing Your love and Your Word with an empty soul, let me do it now, before it's too late.

Natural Beauty

What a tremendous sense of beauty You have, heavenly Father! I can't help but marvel every time I get out of the man-made concrete, steel, and glass ghettos in which we live.

I don't have to go far. Just to step outside at night is enough . . . to see the stars and realize how our whole world is less than a drop in the bucket in Your vast universe. Or just to take out a microscope, to see what worlds lie hidden in each drop of water, in each living cell.

The miracle of life—how beautiful! We can mathematically harness the laws of nature and put men on the moon, but we can't create even so much as a blade of grass that lives and grows.

We can tap the secrets and learn to use the forces You put in the world, but we can't make them.

Through the centuries the world and all of nature cry out: "There is one God! Great and mighty is He! Bow before Him, and praise His name."

Let me ever see Your fingerprints in nature, Father, so I too will ever sing, "How great Thou art!"

My Pastor

Lord Jesus, bless my pastor. Show me how I can make his work more pleasant.

Don't let me pay too much attention to the inconsequentials, like his age and mannerisms. Help me remember that He is working for You and that He is shouldering pretty heavy responsibilities.

Show me how I can work with him in serving You. For after all, he's supposed to be our leader (right?) and not just someone to work for us.

I think of how much time he spends in chasing down mavericks that run off in all directions, and in doing things we said we'd do but didn't. Man, how much more could be accomplished if he could use that time in building up God's people and in leading others to You.

I thank You for him, Jesus. I recognize him as a special gift You've given us.

Help me love him, respect him, have confidence in him, follow him, encourage him, work with him, pray for him. For somehow it comes through to me that when I am doing all this, I'm really doing it for You.

Before Church

Holy Spirit, I wish I could always say honestly, "I was glad when they said to me, 'Let us go to the house of the Lord!' " Would You give me such joy?

Really, church should be the most wonderful place in the world — "the house of the Lord . . . the place where Your glory dwells."

Maybe we've been looking at it the wrong way and making of it something other than what it should be.

Maybe we think too much about who's going to be there (or why weren't they?) rather than that You are with us there.

Maybe we pay too much attention to how the minister says things rather than listening to the Word he is sharing.

Maybe we're more conscious of ushers and choirs and organ than the act of worship itself.

Holy Spirit, as I now go to church, make me a true worshiper. Let me sense God's presence, sing God's praises, hear God's Word, rejoice in God's forgiving love, offer myself to God's will and guidance, and go home in the peace of God's blessing.

After Church

The service is over. But is it, Father?

We came to be with You. Now You're going out into the world with us.

We came to hear Your Word. Now comes the doing.

Father, no disrespect intended, but it seems to me that church at its best is a little like a locker room before a big game.

The coach is there, pepping everybody up and reminding them why they're there. He gives them instructions and warnings, and then sends them out on the field.

He's out there with them to encourage them on. He's really running the game. His word keeps coming through, and the regular huddles keep the team together as they push their way down the field.

Father, church is over. I'm out on the field now. Don't let me forget what You said to me or whose side I'm on. Help us encourage one another in family huddles and friend huddles so we gain ground during the week instead of losing it.

For life is a game to be won — not just played.

Baptism

You know, Father, I should think about something as important as Baptism much more than I do.

I guess I don't because it's already happened and doesn't ever have to be repeated. And probably also because it looks like such a simple act.

There's a promise and water and a blessing — and that's it. That's the way it appears.

But Father, don't ever let me forget that what You do in that simple act makes it one of the most important moments in our lives.

You actually give us a whole new life, a being born again of water and the Spirit. You wash us completely so that we are new and clean.

Help me keep this is mind every day. For every day I ought to come to You, asking You to keep me clean and to help me really be that new person in Christ.

I thank You for what You did for me in Baptism. Now, Father, help me keep my baptismal promise till I die.

Before Communion

Loving Savior, I truly want to come to Your Table, to take part in this Holy Communion.

I almost hesitate to come. I know how I have sinned against You. Every day I let You down in so many ways that it almost seems out of place to come and ask for Your blessing.

But I'm coming anyway, because I believe You meant it when You said You would never turn away anyone who comes to You. I'm coming as someone who is really sorry about my wrongs. I ask only that You forgive.

But I'm coming happily too. Because I know Your love. I know that by Your death You have taken away my sin — and everyone else's too.

Lord, may Your body and blood make me strong — in faith, in the joy and peace of being forgiven, in love to You and others.

Let me go home as one who has been personally reminded of what it's all about. Let my life the rest of the week show I don't forget.

After Communion

Dearest Jesus, I thank You for this most wonderful gift You brought me in such a personal way—
. . . Your body and blood, given and shed for the remission of all my sins,
. . . the joy of forgiveness,
. . . the peace of Your pardon.

Sometimes I feel as if my life were glaring, ugly words scrawled with a grease pencil on a clean sheet of paper. I don't like what it says about me.

Then You come and touch a flame to the paper, and right before my eyes it disappears. The ugliness isn't there anymore, thanks to You.

Jesus, I joyously thank You for taking my sin away and for reassuring me of my being forgiven in this Communion. But I ask now for Your patient help.

You've told others: "Your sins are forgiven. Now go and sin no more." But I know well enough I won't make it. I'll sin again before this day is over.

Please, Lord, forgive again—and again—and again.

And make me a stronger Christian, that my life may be more what You want it to be.

II

Discovering Me

Capital I

Dear Jesus, help me find myself and be myself.

Sometimes I feel real down. I think I could slip out of this world and no one would care — or even notice.

Then again at times I feel as if the whole world is revolving around me — and that it really should.

It's a little like the word "I." Whenever I write about myself, I always capitalize "I." Yet it's such a tiny word that it never sticks out offensively unless I blow it all out of proportion.

I do have real importance. You've told me I mean enough to You that You even know me by my name . . . that You died for me personally . . . that You've prepared a place just for me with You in heaven . . . that You hear my every prayer, even though You have a whole world's cares to attend to.

Yet You've turned right around and showed me that I shouldn't feel myself more important than others, that I shouldn't love myself more than I love others. No, it's better the way You put it — I should love others as I love myself!

I am important. They are too — even the least of them. Help me catch and keep this point of view.

Good Morning, Lord!

Good morning, Lord! Thank You for a good night's sleep! Thank You for keeping us all safely through this night!

The delicious feel of bed, of yawns and stretches, makes me want to sleep in. You're giving us a new day, and I'm anxious to make the most of it.

Lord, as You have been with me through these hours of darkness, keep me with You through these hours of light. Let every word I speak, everything I do, my every thought and attitude show I am with You.

Let nothing on my part this day bring discredit to my name, or to my family's, or to Yours.

Help me see Your guiding and blessing hand, and give me enough spirit of adventure to leave the ruts and nowheres, where so many are content to lag, and follow where You lead.

Make me gloriously alive in every moment of this day, and may the glory of it ever be Yours.

Good Night, Lord!

Now that this day is almost over, Lord, I want to spend a few more moments with You, before I say good night.

It has been a pretty good day. The way You've guided and provided, I owe You a lot of thanks. I'd have to be blind not to see it and dead inside not to respond gratefully.

Not everything has been as I would have wanted it. But if it made me sense my need of You and made me turn to You, it has been good.

I haven't been all I wanted to be either. I regret some of the things I did and said, and I confess that some of my attitudes were unbecoming a Christian.

I want You to know I really care. I'm sorry about it all, Lord. I need Your love to give me clean heart and hands again, and to help me do better tomorrow.

But while I'm asking You to forgive, I'm deep down happy in knowing Jesus' forgiving love. And I know I'm safe in that love.

So I sleep in peace — tonight and every night. Good night, Lord! And thank You!

Wonderful Me

Heavenly Father, when I look in a mirror, I can get pretty excited about what I see.

Now don't get me wrong! I don't mean that I'm stuck on myself. What I mean is what David said: "I am wonderfully made."

I look at my eyes and marvel that those little balls of tissues and liquids can give me a constant picture of all the beauty and form and movement and color of all around me. And in 3-D yet!

I look at my tongue, that crazy little flexible muscle tied down on only one end, and marvel how, along with my lips and voice, it can make the thousands of slightly different sounds that end up as understandable language.

I look at my ears and marvel at the range of sounds that make up the noise I hear and the music I enjoy.

I look at my skin and marvel that You have wrapped me in such a unique protective covering — so tough and flexible that it can take blows and bruises, yet so soft that even holding hands is fun.

No, Father, the mirror doesn't fill me with vanity or make me wonder about some kind of evolution. It makes me realize what a wonderful God You must be to make such a wonderful me!

"Childish Ways"

"When I was a child, I spoke like a child, I thought like a child, I reasoned like a child; when I became a man, I gave up childish ways."

Lord, I guess I'm not completely adult yet. But I'm getting pretty close to it.

I no longer enjoy little kid stuff. I've grown out of childish things and childish ways.

Oh, sure, at times I wish I were small again. Little children have it pretty soft—playing most of the time, having someone else solve their problems and take away their hurts.

But it's good being able to see more and figure things out for myself; and making decisions; and standing on my own feet; and knowing You personally as my Savior; and believing because I'm sure it's so.

Lord, don't ever let me stop growing and maturing—in spirit as well as in mind and body.

Yet, let me never lose a child's faith and love. For I remember You also said, "Unless you become like children, you will never enter the kingdom of heaven."

Beauty Is Only Skin?

Father, sometimes I feel like hiding.

I'm like everybody else. I'd like to feel attractive, to have people think I really look neat.

There are so many beautiful people around. I envy them their smooth skin, their well-shaped bodies, their pleasant voices and graceful ways. Not bad envy, Father. I just wish I were like them.

But I also know it's not true that "beauty is only skin deep." There are some who come in pretty packaging who don't have much inside. And some of the very beautiful people in this world come in plain wrappers.

You know, I don't even have the slightest idea what Jesus looked like. But He was really beautiful!

So Father, don't let me get too self-conscious about pimples and cracking voice, about weight and height.

Just let me try to be a beautiful person, like Jesus. For that is lasting beauty, and it always shows through.

The Facts of Life

Understanding Father, help me understand the changes that are taking place in me.

As my body changes visibly, as new cycles begin, as new feelings arise — help me know what's going on and how to handle it!

I know it's good — though perhaps a little scary at times. This is the way You made us. And like everything You made, You Yourself said it was very good. I agree.

Now Father, I need to know the facts of life, and I want to learn them the right way.

I don't want to make costly mistakes or develop sick attitudes. I've seen fellows bust up cars because they didn't know or care about using them right. I've seen boys and girls bust up their lives because they didn't know or care about what they did.

I also know that the rules of the road are as important as being able to drive. And that the rules and limits You placed on sex are just as important as the biological facts.

Help me avoid a collision course, Father, by understanding, appreciating, respecting, and handling the new me Your way.

Mealtime

Father, I thank You . . .

> . . . for all the different foods with which we can fill up several times every day;
>
> . . . for their good taste as well as that they are good for us;
>
> . . . for being able to taste and enjoy;
>
> . . . for health to eat and to earn our bread;
>
> . . . for good soil, sun and rain, planting and harvest;
>
> . . . for ranchers and farmers, workers and clerks, the long pipeline to our full table;
>
> . . . for loved ones to eat with, so that mealtime is not an hour of silence and loneliness.

Father, use these gifts to bless and strengthen us. And give us love to share Your goodness with others who are missing out in some way or other.

Happiness Is . . .

Happiness is . . . what, heavenly Father?

A big date with No. 1, and permission to stay out till midnight?

A USC-Notre Dame football game in color?
A set of wheels that is all my own?

Father, I know there are millions who have no place to go; who have no TV or comfortable home; who would have no gas or roads even if they did have a car.

For them happiness is a hot meal . . . a room, pillow, and blanket . . . a pair of shoes . . . a chance to go to school.

Maybe happiness is even simpler than that: knowing someone loves you . . . knowing that after a good night's sleep, there'll be another chance tomorrow . . . hope . . . accomplishment.

Or isn't it still deeper, Father? Knowing You love me . . . You will still bless me tomorrow, even though I let You down today . . . being sure that Jesus lives, and that I need not fear the future . . . or anything else.

I guess happiness comes with recognizing Your blessings in our lives and being truly grateful for them. Father, make me such a happy person.

Phonies

I don't get it, Father.

There's this woman—the worst gossip around, and really mean to the kids. Yet she's the big wheel in the ladies aid.

And the man at the corner store. He hires teen-agers, makes them work like dogs, and pays them way below minimum because he knows they can't find any other job. He goes to church too.

And some of their members raised a fuss about the congregation's getting too integrated. That's just the way they put it.

Lord, they're phonies, aren't they?

Some say that proves the church has failed. But I know that isn't right. Just because someone claims to follow You but doesn't, doesn't mean that You are not worth following.

I'm glad we still have the church, and I guess it's really good such people also go to church. Maybe something will get through to them. Maybe they'll change.

Father, maybe I'd better look at myself too! I wonder if what others see in me makes them think I'm a phony.

Sex

Holy Father, I'm not sure I ever used the word *sex* in a prayer before. I even feel a little funny doing it now.

Yet I know sex is one of the finest and most beautiful gifts You've given us. If I stutter on the word, it's because I'm conscious of how we humans have dirtied something so clean and good.

I know that sex is life and love. I'm happy I'm old enough to notice the opposite sex and really enjoy their company.

And that feeling of love. It's hard to describe, but I really like it. I thank You for it.

Now don't let me forget that this is all a part of Your goodness to me. Don't let me play around with Your gift in ways that You never intended.

You've warned, "Flee youthful lusts." Help me avoid talk and jokes and dates that make sex cheap and distasteful.

Real love is too wonderful and respect for each other is too much a part of it to let me take a chance on spoiling it by fooling around.

"Create in me a clean heart, O God," and help me keep it clean.

Pot

Lord, wake us all up to what a serious problem we have, what with so many turning to pot. It's not just that they're using marijuana or pills or even stronger drugs. It's that they feel they have a perfect right to do it.

Cigarettes aren't in very much anymore. Most kids now steer clear, because they don't want to get wiped out by lung cancer.

But why don't they use the same sense when it comes to grass and acid, and uppers and downers, and all the rest of the junk? Even if they like feeling high, can't they see what it has done to others and where it could lead them?

Help them, Lord. And help me. Almost every day temptation is there. Someone is always around to say, "How do you know what it's like until you try it?" Strengthen me so I don't give in.

And what can I do about them, Lord? Besides pray? We all hate to squeal. But if we all put the finger on where it is and where it's coming from, wouldn't a lot of the mess clear up in a hurry? And wouldn't we be protecting many who haven't been hurt yet? And helping others who have?

Wouldn't that be love in action? Lord, give me the courage to do what I can before it's too late.

Money

Father, they keep telling me, "Money doesn't grow on trees." I know that. If it did, I'd have planted one long ago.

But it's true, we don't all see eye to eye on money. To me money is what you spend to get what you want when you want it. Parents talk about investments and security and obligations and the future.

Father, help us understand one another better. I know they're much wiser by experience. But I'd also like them to know I'm not completely irresponsible.

I don't want them to pamper me with generous handouts—though I'll take them when they're offered. I'd rather earn by my own effort—whether it's an outside job or just carrying some of the weight around the house.

And Father, teach me to use wisely what I have. I know I have a lot to learn.

Yes, I'll make mistakes. But when I do, make me mature enough to try to pay for them myself. And make me wise enough not to make the same mistake umpteen times.

Changing Tastes

Father, I know what I like. I also know there are many who don't like what I like. I just wish they wouldn't get uptight about it all.

Styles of clothes and music change. What I like now I probably won't like two years from now. It's no big deal.

I'm not defending dressing and acting like a weirdo. Or looking like the bathtub hadn't been invented. Or behaving as if there were no Ten Commandments. Or tearing up the neighborhood with electric guitars on full volume.

But if I like the sound and beat of now music — there's nothing wrong with it, is there? And if some folk songs make me feel closer to You — that's good, isn't it?

I don't mean that this is the way it should be for everybody, that the churches should junk great music and hymns and meaningful and beautiful ways and traditions, or change Your message to suit us.

We'd all be losers if that happened.

All I ask is the chance to enjoy what I like, as long as there's nothing wrong with it. And that I do it without being inconsiderate of others or their getting down on me.

Wheels

Lord, can I talk to You about wheels for a moment? I need Your help to keep me thinking straight.

There's something exciting about speed and power —the squeal of rubber, the roar of a juiced-up engine. And the feel of having one's own car is really great.

What I need to ask, Lord, is that You keep me mindful that while I'm playing around with a new toy, I'm also handling a potentially deadly weapon.

I hear others talking about getting totaled out. They act as if the only tragedy is having to wait until they get a new set of wheels.

But I know little kids have been killed or crippled by some who think kicks is dragging down a city street. What then? A thousand "I'm sorrys" or anything else will never undo that terrible hurt and loss.

I'm happy I've reached an age where cars and driving are a part of my thing.

Now make me a responsible driver. Let me remember "Thou shalt not kill" every time I hit the road.

Of Screen and Tube

Lord Jesus, I wish these were Your years on earth. I'll bet You would enjoy movies and television. They entertain and put a point across in such an interesting and great way.

But I'll bet You'd shed many a tear over them too. Maybe not over them — over us.

Film producers say they make what people pay to see. They claim that young people are their bread and butter. If the trend in movies then is to shocking violence and sordid sex, what does that say about us? Is that what we really want?

I don't. But I'm not sure I let my feelings come out as clearly as I should.

The industry is fair to me. They even rate their own pictures, so I can be choosy. Now it's up to me — to be fair to them and true to myself and You.

It shouldn't have to be a matter of parents approving or disapproving. Or the theater's being tight or loose about enforcing restrictions. It's up to me.

Lord Jesus, I am Yours. By Your love, by what You did for me, by faith, I am Yours. Let everything, including my choice of entertainment, show I am.

The Pressure's On!

Father, I wish I could just lie out in the sun without getting disturbed — to relax, to dream, to think about everything.

So much of the time I'm uptight about something or other. It seems the pressure's always on.

But why do I have to feel I'm competing in everything I do? Am I supposed to feel guilty or a lesser person if I don't make the team or get the best grades, or if I'm not one of the most popular kids on campus?

I don't like being yelled at either — by students or teachers who tell me what I'm supposed to think or do. And I don't like the pressure of TV — which suggests I'm not with it if I don't dress far out or think that weird visuals and loud noise and flashing lights are groovy.

Father, I remember how Jesus considered it important to get away from it all, to rest and think and pray awhile. A person just can't see straight when he's all steamed up, or walk straight when he's pushed around.

Open the pressure valves in my life, Father. Take away the tightness, so I can make up my own mind after really thinking and talking things through quietly with You.

When I'm Sick

Lord Jesus, let me feel Your presence in this sickroom. Make me patient and strong enough to bear this burden, which is a little too heavy for me.

I'm not really afraid, for I know You are with me. But I'm finding out how weak I am, how much I need Your loving care.

I don't doubt Your power to heal me. What I need is small compared to the needs of the blind, the deaf, the dumb, the crippled and crazed who reached out their arms to You. You healed them all, even when their cases seemed hopeless. I know You'll have me on my feet in no time too.

I need to remember that if You love me so much that You died to heal me of the cancer of sin, You won't ever let me down.

So keep my eyes on You, and my faith strong. Use this illness to draw me closer to You, to teach me what it means to trust.

Muddling Through

Dear Jesus, help me make the most of my life.

You've given me so much. But there's such a temptation to waste it, to let it all slip through my fingers.

I'm inclined to gear my life to what I see in others. I'm content as long as I know I'm doing as well as they are. I'm ready to have my life graded by the curve system.

But why? Why should I muddle through when I could go so far ahead? Why should I be satisfied with low performance?

We criticize the world and church for not doing a better job. But how could either one of them do much of a job when so many who are blessed with extraordinary gifts are content to be so very ordinary?

Let me learn from You, Lord, how to live fully. In everything You did, You gave the very best. In little things, whether teaching or helping individuals, no one could ever do more than You. In big things, like saving the whole world, You gave Your all.

Lord Jesus, don't let me muddle and piddle, when there could be so much more to my life.

Doing One's Own Thing

Father, as You well know, a lot of kids my age are rebels. There's a lot of noise about how everyone should be completely free to do his or her own thing.

It sounds great. I too believe personal freedom is one of the best gifts You've given us. But sometimes I get confused. Who's free? When is one free?

Some of us are sold on our country, even though we know our government isn't perfect. We believe in following Jesus as the only way of happy life, and in Jesus as the Way to eternal life. We like to dress up and clean up, and we feel that there is a constant need for law and order.

But there are those who say we've sold out to the establishment, that we're slaves of tradition, when we're honestly doing our thing.

Father, I believe in freedom. I'd stand and fight to be free. But I'm convinced that, as Jesus said, freedom comes from truth, and that the standard of truth is You and Your Word, and that Christ, in His love, has really made us free.

Father, don't let me get mixed up. Help me show others, whose thing isn't worth doing, where freedom really lies.

Words

Father, I thank You for words. It's a real blessing to be able to get feelings and thoughts across to others without having to cry or gesture or stamp my foot.

I thank You for intelligence, for being able to understand the ideas we put into the framework of words.

Help me see how important it is to use words carefully, so we can get closer to one another and be more helpful to one another.

Don't let us become like mynah birds in a cage, squawking out words and phrases that are completely irrelevant.

Let words be our way of opening our hearts and minds to one another. For how can we love and help one another if we don't know or understand one another?

I'm so grateful that You, Father, have done so much in communicating with us. I've never seen You, yet I know You — because You've given us a written Word — and because You sent Jesus to be the living Word.

Thank You for getting Your message across to me in such a wonderful way.

When I'm on Top of It

Father, some days everything goes right. No matter what happens, I seem to be on top of it. And what a glorious feeling it is!

There's only one thing wrong. On days like that I'm so busy enjoying myself, I sometimes forget to say thanks. Not always, fortunately. But far too often.

I ask, Father, that I may learn not to take Your goodness and the kindness of others for granted.

If I got only what I deserve, I'd have a pretty empty life. But, Father, You keep filling my cup so it runs over. You send more than I need.

If horizons seem to wall in and limit my life, help me realize that's only how it looks to me from where I stand — and that some day You'll put me on higher ground, and I'll see much more.

Don't ever let me forget, Father, that when I'm on top of it, it's all because of You.

When I'm Out of It

Father, some days I just feel out of it.

Nothing looks good. I don't seem to have any pep, any ambition. I just lie around feeling sorry for myself and making everyone else mad.

Why, Father?

You made the world so beautiful . . . and life so rich and wonderful. I really haven't anything to gripe about.

Snap me out of it, Father. Don't let my moods ruin my days and make other people wish they didn't know me.

And don't let me blame everyone else for the sour way I feel.

Keep me interested in something. Not just anything, but something worthwhile — that my life may not become empty because I let its fullness leak away.

What Shall I Be?

Everybody asks that, Father — my counselor, teachers, relatives, friends. It's almost always the same question.

I'm not sure I'm ready to answer it yet. Some things sound pretty good now. But will they a few years from now when I know what all goes into it? when I get an actual taste of it?

I'm sure You will show me what to do with my life, Father. You made me. You programed me for something worthwhile. I know You will help me discover what it is.

One thing! As I look ahead, don't let me view work as a drag or money as its chief reward. Or a big name as the mark of success.

Keep my sights high. Help me find a place where I can feel I am really doing something worth doing. Whether or not others consider it an important job doesn't matter. And help me find a place where You can also see love and faith in what I'm doing.

But for now, Father, just keep me learning, that when the door opens, I'll be prepared to step in.

Minibrains

Lord Jesus, give me the courage to think for myself.

It's a funny thing. We talk about the establishment and conforming to its standards and rows of little boxes — but are we any different?

Someone decides to be different, and everyone copies. So who's being himself?

Long hair, short hair, maxies, minies — I guess really none of that is the problem, no matter how many argue and fight over it. It's minibrains.

I must admit that a lot of what's happening is neither beautiful nor good. It's just a mark of rebellion. It's not for anything. It's just against.

It's our thing. It shows who we are. It sets us apart.

But sometimes I wonder how this all looks to You. Because You're as much concerned about the why as the what — perhaps even more.

Lord, teach me to think — and to think for myself. Don't let me mindlessly do what others do just so I feel in.

I know it takes strength and courage to be myself. But anything less is too little.

Many Thanks!

Thank You, Father, for Your overwhelming love.

I thank You . . .
     . . . for just letting me be alive and around —
     and for promising and giving an even
     better life in Christ;
     . . . for the power to grow physically, spiri-
     tually, mentally, socially — so that I can
     tomorrow be a little healthier, wiser,
     stronger than I am today;
     . . . for parents who not only had me but
     lovingly provided and guided — and still
     do;
     . . . for a family and friends who taught me
     that forgiving is a part of loving;
     . . . for Your willingness to forgive me and for
     sending Your Son to be my Savior;
     . . . for challenges and opportunities, for
     dreams and plans;
     . . . for calm and storm, for fun and work, for
     sleep and excitement, for joy and sorrow.

Yes, Father, I thank You for them all.

For I know that You use them all for good to those
who love You.

III

*Family,
Friends,
and School*

To Be a Family

Dear Father in heaven, help me appreciate what it means to be part of a family.

It just has to mean more to me than a group tied together by blood and name, and kept together in one house. There have to be love and the readiness for all to live for one another.

All living for one another. Father, that's the point that's so easy to forget.

Sometimes some of us want to keep getting but never give anything in return. We like being loved, but we're stingy in loving back.

I guess I, at times, take my family for granted too. I act as if it's Mother's duty to cook and clean for me, and Dad's to keep me supplied with what I need and want. But why should they?

They do it though. But not because they owe it to me. I know it's because they love me.

Father, since I'm lucky enough to be a part of this family, maybe it's time I explore how I can put more love into it too. There are many things I can do, many ways to make life more pleasant for the rest, as well as for me.

Help me show that my family means something to me by making me a responsible part of it.

My Parents

Dear Jesus, teach me how to love my parents.

I do appreciate them, even though I don't always show it. I want them to know how grateful I am — not just for what they do for me but for what they are.

I hurt them so often. I don't want to. I know that's not the way of loving. But sometimes the sharp word slips out, and the stupid act, before I've thought through what would happen.

Lord Jesus, forgive me for causing them hurt and worry. Make me mature enough to ask for their forgiveness.

I know my parents are not perfect. Neither were Yours. Of course, I'm not either. But You are, and You always were. So make me more like You.

When You were at the age — a little like I am now — the age of asking questions and startling others who hadn't realized how much You really knew, You quietly obeyed Your parents. Willingly, too. Even on the cross, You were concerned more about Your mother than Yourself.

Dear Jesus, make me more like You.

They Don't Understand

Heavenly Father, sometimes I wish my parents could understand me the way You do.

But then, how could they? As God, You see behind every mask and closed door. You penetrate into even the deepest secrets of my mind. You know the real me.

Others see mostly what I want them to see and hear what I want them to hear. But not You. You know me even better than I know myself.

But do You know, Father, sometimes my parents also amaze me with their insight. When they look me in the eye, they're not fooled at all. Sometimes when I complain, "They don't understand me!" I fear they understand me only too well. I sense I'm not going to get away with what's on my mind.

But Father, I need their understanding. Only when they know my real feelings and desires and problems can they truly help. And I still do need their help and love.

So push me out of my secret corner. Make my parents willing to give me the time I need, and me willing to open up and level with them.

Then we'll all enjoy a happier home and life, the way You intended it to be.

Honoring Father and Mother

Lord Jesus, don't ever let me feel that I've outgrown my need of honoring my parents.

I don't just mean to the extent of loving them. I mean also respecting them and obeying them. Without resenting it. Or begrudging it.

When I don't feel like it, remind me of You. The Bible says You were "obedient to them." Not only to Your heavenly Father. Also to Your earthly parents.

I know You knew more than Mary and Joseph. I keep thinking that because of who You were, it should have been the other way around. They should have obeyed You.

But You came to fulfill the Law, not break it. Isn't that the way You put it? You came to be a perfect Person for us — as also our Savior, of course.

Jesus, when I'm at my best I'm most like You. Let me be that way with my father and mother. Let me make their lives happier by showing how much I love and respect them, even if they're not perfect.

The Last Word

Father, I've reached an age where I like to make my own decisions and do things because I want to—not because someone tells me to. That's not bad, is it?

But sometimes this causes trouble. I clash with others—often my parents—and it's not a happy situation. Help them see that I must learn to think for myself. Help me so I don't give them the idea that I'm just trying to be rebellious.

Because really, I don't feel that because I'm a teen-ager I should now be the boss. I don't have all the answers. I know I'm not always right. I realize they would not be using their God-given sense if they just let me have my way.

And when two reach an impasse, I know final authority should not be determined by who can yell loudest, make himself most disagreeable, or threaten most damage. We're all plain stupid if we knuckle under to bully tactics.

Sometimes it's hard, though, to agree who should have his way—who does the straightest thinking or has the best answers.

But Father, make us all wise enough to see that finally You are the One who should have the last word. Get us in the habit of looking to You for those answers that are right for all of us.

Family Oneness

O Holy Spirit, make our family more fully one in Christ.

We believe. In time of trouble we can get right down to sharing our faith with one another. But why does it so often take crisis to get us to spend more time in praying together?

We run our separate ways so much of the time. Our lives are split by school and work, by TV and sports, by clubs and dates and parties. Even PTA and church meetings play into the picture more than they should.

We just aren't together enough — I mean, really doing things together, things that matter.

Holy Spirit, teach us how to make better use of our togetherness. To make sure we take a little time each day when we put everything else aside just to be together, and to be together with You . . . when we can listen to what You say to us in Your Word and talk about it in a way that it helps us all.

Lord, make us more fully one. In every way. In our Christian faith too.

My Friends

Lord Jesus, I know Your promise, "I am with you always," and I know You are with me.

But I need other friends too. Not a lot. Just a few whom I can feel close to and trust. A few whose company I can really enjoy.

I know good friends don't just happen. I have to be one to have one.

I realize also that it's important what kind of friends I have. No friend is worth having if he leads me away from You or tempts me to do what I know is wrong.

I thank You for those friends with whom I can really have fun without feeling sorry about anything afterwards.

And I ask You to lead me to more such friends — the kind where You, Jesus, can be a part of the group without anyone feeling we've suddenly become a crowd.

People

Heavenly Father, help me see people the world over as fellow human beings.

Don't let their strange languages, strange customs, strange dress, strange diet, and strange beliefs keep me from seeing them as real persons.

They hurt like I hurt and laugh like I laugh. They have dreams and plans, hopes and ambitions, just as I do. They need love as I do. Their friends and loved ones mean as much as mine do to me.

They need You and Your love as I do. When Jesus died and rose, He didn't intend that victory for just certain races or nations. That love is for all — for them as for me.

So don't let me look at others who are different and feel superior to them because they don't have all I have. Rather let me be concerned that they be given more opportunity, and let me personally reach out a warm and helpful hand.

Teach me to seek out and find a brotherly oneness with all whose paths cross mine — that we may be able to understand one another, care about one another, help one another. Wherever possible, let the love of Jesus make our bond all the deeper and more real.

Togetherness

Father, there's so much togetherness in our lives
that isn't really togetherness at all.

Cruising up and down a few blocks on Main
Street Friday and Saturday nights — all lanes
jammed with every breed of stock and customized
cars — everyone gawking at everyone else who
inches by.

Parties where no one really pays any attention
to anyone else — everyone just milling around and
moving to the beat.

Crowds that fill the pews — most unaware of one
another — warm greetings being offered mostly
to and by the pastor — friends seeking friends
and ignoring the others.

Make our moments of togetherness meaningful.

Make them really count for something —
    by touching each other's hearts,
    not just rubbing elbows;
    by sharing the love of Christ,
    not just time and space.

Dates

Father, I'm going out on a date again. Thank You for helping me find such special friends—with whom I can really be myself and have a good time.

I am grateful, too, that my parents don't tease or make fun of it. I don't mind their checking on who I'll be with or where we'll be going or what we'll be doing. They have a right to know. After all, love wants to be sure everything's right.

Help me set their minds at ease by letting them know that we won't forget that You are with us all the time and that we won't do anything that isn't right in Your sight.

Now, Father, I ask You to watch over us. Don't let anything happen to mar our pleasure. Don't let us do stupid things to try to impress each other. Help us enjoy each other's company honestly, just being ourselves—being our Christian selves.

School — Yeuch!

Heavenly Father, all my life I've been doing nothing but going to school. It gets to be a terrible drag.

When I see all the exciting things there are to do in the world, I can sympathize with dropouts. Who wants to be old before you begin living? Any kind of change seems welcome.

But don't worry, Father. Though I sound and am impatient, I won't do anything foolish.

I know this is get-ready time. I'm not yet prepared to handle the complexities of life or to hold down the kind of job I'd like to have.

So, Father, don't let me waste these years fighting school. Help me zero in on what I want my life to be. Give me big plans and ambitions. And show me how a lot of what I'm learning is helping me towards those goals.

I guess I should also thank You for school, Father. It's pretty great to have a dream, almost any dream, and find that someone's there to train you for it.

I do thank You, Father. Now help me make the most of these years.

My Teachers

Bless my teachers, Lord Jesus.

They may have their different ways. Some get through to me better than others. Some I really don't like much at all.

But there's one thing I have to say for them all. They care enough about others, especially young people, that they were willing to prepare for and spend their lives in teaching us.

Make them wise, Lord, in more than the subject they teach. And keep them honest, so they won't mislead us by presenting theory as if it were proven fact or speculation as if it were truth.

Make them as ready to learn as they are to teach. Give them a willingness to learn from You, for like wise Solomon said, "The fear of the Lord is the beginning of wisdom."

Let my attitudes be such that their job may be more pleasant. Let my interest be such that they find satisfaction in teaching me.

Fill me with such appreciation and respect for them that they may be grateful they became teachers.

Vacation

O Father, what a wonderful feeling it is to break out of the daily rut. I guess You made us that way, where every so often we need a change.

Just like with Your making a Lord's day — the Sabbath, a day of rest. You said it should be a day set aside for You. You said You didn't want us to work as usual on that day. It's not that You needed it. We do — to get rested, refreshed, strengthened, retooled for the rest of the week.

Father, I pray my vacation may do that for me too. This is a chance to do some of the many things I've wanted to do but never had time for. A chance to get out in Your wide, wonderful world and see a little of Your glory.

Don't let me waste my vacation, Father. There's so much to see and do — things that will bring me closer to You, not draw me away from You; things that will help me grow as a Christian while I'm enjoying rest, fun, and a real change.

This could be my best vacation ever, Father. Help me make it that.

IV

*For
Everything
There Is
a Time*

Ecclesiastes 3

A Time to Be Born

Heavenly Father, I guess the greatest gift in life has to be life itself.

The way I celebrate my birthdays, with everybody congratulating me and giving me presents, would make it seem as if I had something to do with being born. But I know I didn't. Life is all a gift — from You, through my parents.

It's the same with my being a Christian. I'm real happy about being spiritually alive. So is everyone else who knows what life in Christ is all about.

I know that this too is all a gift. It is a matter of having been "born again, of water and the Spirit." It is Your love, working a new life in me. It's not something I decided to be or do.

How thankful I should be! Every time I enjoy anything — absolutely anything — I should remember I wouldn't be enjoying it at all if You hadn't first given me life.

Thank You, Father! You've given me life. Let me live it joyously! You've given me new life in Christ. Let each day find me excitingly alive to You!

A Time to Die

Lord Jesus Christ, most of us don't like to talk or think about death very much.

We see a lot of death in movies and TV, as one after another is zapped right out of the story, but it doesn't really do anything to us. We can walk away from it and forget it.

But it's different in real life. Every so often a loved one dies, or a friend in school. And it hurts, and there's no walking away or forgetting.

I really feel sorry for those who don't know You. There aren't any answers for them, or any hope or peace.

I don't know what I'd do if I didn't have You. The way You said, "I am the Resurrection and the Life; he that believes in Me, though he were dead, yet shall he live," and then turned right around and proved it by raising dead Lazarus — now that's something to hold on to!

The way You died for us, and then came out of the grave a heroic Conqueror — and Your promise, "Because I live, you shall live also" — that takes away the hurt and fear!

Let me never forget — death is real — but You are even more real! So is the eternal life You offer and give!

A Time to Plant

Father, every so often I hear someone say: "Do you know what's wrong with young people today? They want everything for nothing." But Father, that's not fair.

Yes, we do get a lot for nothing — maybe too much. But if they're foolish enough to give it, we're smart enough to take it. But that doesn't mean we want it this way.

Don't let their foolishness — or ours — cheat us out of learning the joy of planting.

I know that planting means hard work. It's all giving, with the getting end of it a long way off in the future.

But how sweet it is to taste the bread of our own sweat. How satisfying to see something good and know we've been partly responsible for it.

I know that was even Jesus' way of doing things. His whole life was a planting. Every parable, every miracle — really everything He said and did was sowing seed. I see even His death as part of the planting process. It was all a giving to bring about a rich harvest in heaven.

Lord, teach me the joy of planting — of giving out of myself. And give me patience to wait for the reward.

A Time to Reap

Let's face it, Father! This is what most of us are waiting for—"the time to pluck up what is planted." The time of harvest, of getting. The time of enjoying what we've been working for.

But then, that's the way it should be, isn't it? This is a time of joy. It's what makes everything else very worthwhile.

Like our being saved! That's the reason why Jesus' life and death cannot be considered waste. That's why angels sang when Jesus came to be one of us. They saw what His coming would accomplish. They foresaw the joy of harvest as the seeds were being sown.

If there were no possible gain, why would Jesus have come? or taken so much guff? or died? Why would anyone work? Why should they?

It's hope that makes us plant seeds. Hope gets us to make plans and then work those plans. In hope we tell of Christ and try to serve.

Father, let me look forward to the joy of reward. You know that's not my only reason for doing. But it is an incentive—and a good one.

When Your love provides such joy, why shouldn't I be happy about it?

A Time to Break Down

Heavenly Father, I remember . . .

   . . . how You once, by a flood, washed out a world made evil and ugly by its own sin;

   . . . how You threatened to destroy, and actually did destroy, whole cities that laughed off decency;

   . . . how Jesus lashed out against those that were making a den of thieves out of Your house of prayer.

There is a time to break down; isn't there, Father?

When wrong is accepted as right . . .
When traditional ways no longer mean what they should . . .
When prejudices prevent some from receiving what they have a perfect right to have . . .
When petty interests stymie great possibilities . . .
. . . it has to be a time to break down.

But Father, let me remember there's a difference between breaking down and annihilating. Jesus cleansed the temple. He didn't burn it down.

Don't let me be foolish enough to throw away the good with the bad, or nothing will be left.

A Time to Build Up

This is harder, Father.

It's easier to tear down
    than to build up.
It's easier to gripe about a problem
    than to find a way to solve it.
It's easier to criticize and condemn
    than to help constructively.
It's easier to shout about what I'm against
    than to stand up for what I'm for.

You, Father, cracked down on sin,
    but then You sent us a Savior from sin.
You sternly warned, "The soul that sins shall die,"
    but then You offered life through Christ.

Father, make Your ways my ways. Make me ready
to build up, to strengthen, to encourage, to work
alone and with others, for good.

I can't do what You have done. Nor am I asking to
build lasting monuments. Just use me so that
something may be a little better than it was before
I came.

A Time to Weep

There is a time for tears, Father, isn't there? There are moments when we just can't keep from crying, no matter how we try. Jesus Himself wept.

But I recall also that Jesus warned that we too often weep for the wrong reason.

We weep at death. But should we? When we really believe that all who fall asleep in Jesus will ever be with their loving Lord?

We cry when we lose money or a job or friends, or when we fail a course, or when we get punished for doing something wrong. But should we? Maybe we ought to think about whether You're trying to tell us something.

I really should weep for those who don't know You, who have no hope or life in Christ, who don't know where they're going or what life is really all about.

I really should have tears for those—perhaps also me—who do know but don't live the faith they claim to have.

Father, help me see things straight until that day when You will wipe all tears from our eyes.

A Time to Laugh

Father, I've been criticized so often for not taking things seriously enough. It's such a welcome relief to have You say, ''There is a time to laugh.''

I pray that I may not flippantly laugh off what is truly serious or find sick amusement in others' misfortunes and handicaps.

I pray that I may not enjoy telling stories that make fun of You or of my faith or of anyone else's convictions, or jokes that dirty up Your beautiful gifts of love and sex.

But Father, I want to laugh! There's so much joy in my life, and You put it all there!

Ever since Jesus was born in Bethlehem so long ago, joy overshadows everything else. I don't ever want to stop singing about it.

Christ has overpowered everything that could hurt me. I know He had to pay a high price for my forgiveness. But He did pay it! He even broke through death for me.

For me! That sounds almost too good to be true! But I know it's true!

Father, You've filled my life with healthy laughter. As I live with You, there's room for little else but joy.

A Time to Embrace

Father, I think I know what You mean. I'm sure You're not talking about dates or necking or anything like that.

You're talking about opening our arms and hearts to other people — isn't that right? Reminding us that You really want us to be like one family and to look on and treat others as if they are our own brothers and sisters — right?

Why is it, Father, that we can brush past people as if they were nothing more than trees or telephone poles? And why do we elbow some out of our lives, because the color of their skin is different . . . or they go to some other church . . . or their parents have less money than ours . . . or they're not very good-looking?

Father, make my life big enough to take everyone in. And, lest brotherhood just be an empty game we play, help us reach the point where we can pray and work together, happy in knowing that we are children of the same heavenly Father.

A Time to Refrain from Embracing

Father, though You made us to be one family, it's pretty clear that it does not always work out that way.

When Jesus came to be Big Brother to all, there were many that disowned Him. Even when He died for them, praying for them, they showed they didn't want anything to do with Him.

Things haven't changed much. People are still choosing up sides and fighting one another and Jesus.

I guess that's why You said that there comes a time when we stop embracing — when we step aside from others so we are not counted or identified with them.

When someone denies You and ridicules my Savior, I don't want anyone to think I'm standing with him. I don't have anything in common with him, and I want him to know it too.

When someone does things You told us not to do, I don't want any part of it.

Yet, Father, even though I can't embrace, I feel You would still want me to pray for him, to be concerned about him, to win him in Christian love.

How do I do it, Father? Show me the way.

A Time to Keep Silence

"It often shows a fine command of language to say nothing."

That puts it pretty well, doesn't it, Father? Sometimes we say too much.

Teach me how to bridle my tongue, to keep it in check, in constant control.

The wrongly spoken word can —
   hurt others, even those I love;
   deceive and mislead;
   turn friends against each other;
   damage another's future;
   turn off the very ones I'm trying to win;
   show that I don't know what I'm talking about.

That's always true — at home too. Sometimes that's where I shoot off my mouth the worst.

A loose tongue can even turn people away from You, Father. It can cause people to say, "If that's the way a Christian talks, I don't want any part of it."

Father, teach me the art of silence. Let my love for You and others show me when it's the right time to keep quiet.

A Time to Speak

Heavenly Father, how often I must disappoint You with my silences.

I disappoint myself. Many is the big chance I missed. I sit there afterwards regretfully asking, "Now why didn't I say something?"

I know why. Sometimes I don't feel sure of myself. I can't think of the right words. Or I'm so angry I don't trust myself. Or I'm afraid I'll be standing alone.

Father, make me stronger so I will speak up more — at the right time and in the right way.

I know that's one of the very things Jesus asks of me. To speak. And to zero in on the most important message of all — Jesus Himself, and His saving love.

He has asked me to tell others about Him so they can get in on His love too, for now and always.

Get me excited about doing it. It's like telling someone that our team won! or that the war is over! or that we've found the perfect Friend, who has a real future for us!

Father, You've given me a tongue, and things to say. You've reminded me there is "a time to speak." Let me find joy in doing it well.

A Time to Love

Father, why is it so hard to love at times? And why am I so inconsistent in showing love to those closest to me, who have done most for me?

Sometimes I feel a little phony about it all. Out in public I'm the perfect one — so obviously considerate of parents and all. But at home I don't always watch what I say or do.

There are times I'm quite ashamed of myself. Yet I try to justify my behavior. "I had a perfect right to do what I did," I say. But that doesn't make me feel any better.

Father, teach me to love Your way —
     . . . even when no one else sees it;
     . . . no matter how much it costs;
     . . . consistently and honestly;
     . . . even when I don't feel like it.

I have good examples to follow —
     . . . Yours, in sending Jesus for all of us, even though most people couldn't care less;
     . . . Christ's, in giving up His life for us, even though none of us deserve such love;
     . . . my parents', in their many sacrifices for me;
     . . . etc., etc., etc.

I know how the game is played. Now help me play it well too.

A Time to Hate

Dearest Jesus, I know the Bible says, "The Lord loves those who hate evil." But I'm not sure I ever paid much attention to those words.

I dislike evil. I've deplored it, regretted it, been turned off by it. I try to avoid it. I even pray daily, "Deliver us from evil." You know I do.

Lord, now teach me to hate evil. Not just in others. In myself too.

When temptation slithers up, let me overcome it by saying, as Joseph did, "How can I do this great wickedness, and sin against God?"

Show me the ugliness of sin. Sin throws blasphemy like garbage in my Father's face. Sin drove nails through Your sinless hands and feet. Sin hurts and kills and destroys all that is good.

Lord Jesus, teach me to hate evil. Help me live and, like the psalm says, "worship in the beauty of holiness."

A Time of War

Almighty Father, I know You are not in favor of war. Killing and crippling and hurting and destroying just are not Your way.

War only shows how stupid, cruel, greedy, and selfish man can be.

But yet there are times when we can't do anything but stand up and fight, aren't there? And that's not ignoring or refusing to do what Jesus said about turning the other cheek.

When a couple of hoods jump on some lady on the street and beat her up, and I just stand there watching, doing nothing to help her, I'm doing wrong. The same goes double if it's my own family getting hurt.

I guess the same thing holds true when one country starts clobbering another. There are times we just have to do something, even if it means war.

Father, I remember that phrase You used — "warring against evil." That's what You want of us, right? No matter if the evil is inside us, or outside. So that it doesn't tear us down and turn us into a bunch of losers.

When evil comes, don't let me knuckle under to it. Give me the will and courage to fight it off. For I too want to wear Christ's victorious crown of life.

A Time of Peace

O heavenly Father, how much we need peace!

Not the peace of holding two fingers in the air, demonstrating with a "Peace" picket sign, and then turning around to hit someone on the head with it.

Not the peace of not caring what happens, or not wanting to get involved in anything.

Father, teach us how to live together . . . to love one another . . . to respect one another . . . to help one another. Show us how to settle our differences unselfishly, to take the chips off our shoulders.

Make us wise enough to see that we can't have peace in this world unless we first have peace in our own family and in ourselves. Unless we really are at peace with You.

The Christmas angels understood how peace comes with Jesus. Now help me understand, at least a little, how Jesus can bring deep and lasting peace to my heart. And Father, help me share Jesus and His peace with others. For when we can kneel together in worship, all loving the same Savior who loves us all, we will find it a little harder to work against one another.

"Grant us Thy peace," Father.

"My peace I give unto you,"
young friend!

— *Jesus Christ*